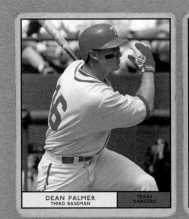
DEAN PALMER
THIRD BASEMAN
TEXAS RANGERS

MARK McLEMORE
SECOND BASEMAN
TEXAS RANGERS

THE STORY OF THE TEXAS RANGERS

Published by Creative Education
P.O. Box 227, Mankato, Minnesota 56002
Creative Education is an imprint of The Creative Company
www.thecreativecompany.us

Design and production by Blue Design
Art direction by Rita Marshall
Printed by Corporate Graphics in the United States of America

Photographs by Getty Images (Brian Bahr, Al Bello/Allsport, B Bennett, Bruce Bennett Studios, Paul K. Buck/AFP, Chris Covatta/Allsport, Jonathan Daniel/Allsport, Diamond Images, Stephen Dunn, Stephen Dunn/Allsport, Otto Greule/Allsport, Harry How, Bob Levey, Brad Mangin/MLB Photos, Ronald Martinez, Jim McIsaac, Doug Pensinger, Rich Pilling/MLB Photos, Louis Requena/MLB Photos, Robert Riger, Rick Stewart/Allsport, Jared Wickerham, John Williamson/MLB Photos, Michael Zagaris/MLB Photos)

Library of Congress Cataloging-in-Publication Data

Gilbert, Sara.
The story of the Texas Rangers / by Sara Gilbert.
p. cm. — (Baseball: the great American game)
Includes index.
Summary: The history of the Texas Rangers professional baseball team from its inaugural 1961 season as the Washington Senators to today, spotlighting the team's greatest players and most memorable moments.
ISBN 978-1-60818-058-5
1. Texas Rangers (Baseball team)—History—Juvenile literature. I. Title. II. Series.

GV875.T4G55 2010
796.357'6409764531—dc22   2010025478

CPSIA: 110310 PO1381

First Edition
9 8 7 6 5 4 3 2 1

Page 3: Infielder Michael Young
Page 4: Right fielder Vladimir Guerrero

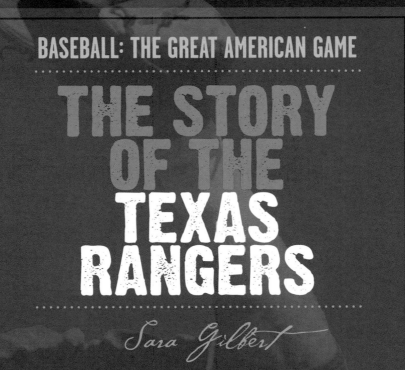

BASEBALL: THE GREAT AMERICAN GAME

THE STORY OF THE TEXAS RANGERS

Sara Gilbert

CREATIVE EDUCATION

CONTENTS

GOING WEST

here are at least 15 cities, towns, and villages named Arlington in the United States. The largest of those is located in northeastern Texas, exactly halfway between the cities of Dallas and Fort Worth. But Texas's Arlington isn't the oldest community of that name. In fact, it was given its name in 1877 in honor of another, older Arlington— the one in Virginia, where Confederate general Robert E. Lee was born. Back then, Arlington, Texas, was a rough-and-tumble frontier outpost. Now it is a bustling, modern city that spreads across 100 square miles and is home to almost 400,000 people and 2 professional sports teams.

Like Lee, who spent several years in Texas in the 1850s defending the frontier against raiding parties of American Indians, Arlington's baseball team has ties to the East Coast—specifically Washington, D.C. When the Washington Senators franchise moved to Minneapolis and became the Minnesota Twins in 1960, Major League Baseball awarded another franchise to Washington, D.C. This team, added to the American League (AL), was again named the Senators, and before

Rangers Ballpark in Arlington (formerly The Ballpark in Arlington) is known as a hitter-friendly park due to its relatively shallow outfield fences.

PITCHER · CHARLIE HOUGH

In 1969, Charlie Hough suffered an arm injury and had to learn a different way to pitch. After Los Angeles Dodgers scout Goldie Holt was done with him, Hough had acquired what became his signature pitch: the knuckleball. During his 10-year tenure in Texas, Hough averaged 15 wins and 240 innings pitched per season. At the peak of his career in 1983, he hurled 3 straight shutouts and threw 37 consecutive scoreless innings. Four years later, the 39-year-old became the oldest pitcher in AL history to lead the league in both starts (40) and total innings pitched (285).

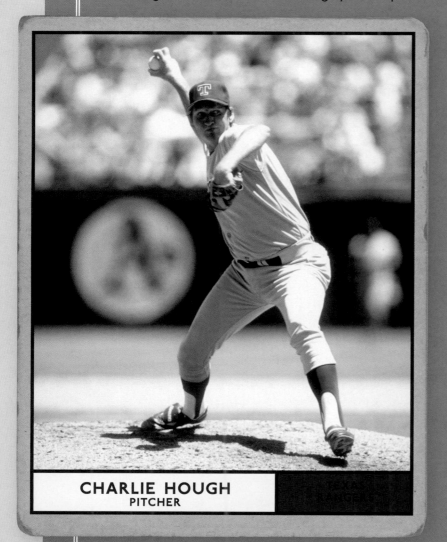

CHARLIE HOUGH
PITCHER

STATS

Rangers seasons: 1980–90

Height: 6-foot-2

Weight: 190

- 2,362 career strikeouts

- 107 career complete games

- 1986 All-Star

- 13 career shutouts

it would become the Texas Rangers in 1972, the team would spend a decade playing ball in the nation's capital.

In hindsight, team owner Elwood "Pete" Quesada probably should have chosen a different name for his new team. The D.C. area had a long history of losing with teams named the Senators, and the newest incarnation of the franchise proved to be no different as it began play in 1961. The Senators posted losing records in eight straight seasons, despite the best efforts of brawny left fielder Frank Howard and catcher Paul Casanova.

While the Senators were struggling, other important events were unfolding that would eventually affect the future of the team. In 1962, Charlie O. Finley, the owner of the Kansas City Athletics, met with AL team owners in New York about moving his team to the Dallas–Fort Worth area—an idea that was ultimately rejected. But 2 years later, construction began on the 10,000-seat Turnpike Stadium in Arlington, slated to be the home of a minor-league team called the Dallas–Fort Worth Spurs.

Back in D.C., legendary Boston Red Sox slugger Ted Williams was hired as manager of the Senators in 1969. Under his guidance, the team posted its first winning record, going 86–76. Pitcher

TED WILLIAMS

Dick Bosman turned in an impressive season, ending with a league-best 2.19 earned run average (ERA), and Howard hit 48 home runs. Williams earned the 1969 AL Manager of the Year award for his efforts, and Senators fans began dreaming of bigger things.

Unfortunately, the Senators would have only that small taste of success to carry them through the next few seasons. They were back under .500 in 1970 and closed 1971 at a dismal 63–96. Interest in baseball had waned in D.C., and not only because the city had a losing team.

FRANK HOWARD

JOHN F. KENNEDY

Every U.S. president but one (Jimmy Carter) since 1910 has thrown at least one ceremonial first pitch, either for opening day, a World Series game, or the All-Star Game. John F. Kennedy did so three times, all for Senators games.

THE LONGEST NIGHT

What did Washington Senators and Chicago White Sox players have in common after a June 12–13 game in 1967? Nearly seven hours of baseball and a lot of explaining to do to their families about just where they had been. When the game started at 8:00 P.M. in D.C. Stadium, no one planned for it to go extra frames. But at the end of the ninth, the game was tied 4–4. Chicago pulled ahead in the 10th, but a wild pitch by Sox hurler Bob Locker and a sacrifice fly during the Senators' half of the inning tied it back up. The clock kept ticking as both teams were stymied for the next 11 innings. Finally, in the bottom of the 22nd inning, the stalemate ended. An exhausted White Sox pitching staff walked two batters and allowed one single. Then, Senators catcher Paul Casanova (pictured) singled to left, driving in a run and ending the contest with a 6–5 victory. The game finally ended at 2:43 in the morning—6 hours and 38 minutes after it began. That game led the league to set a curfew on long-running games. Since then, no inning has been allowed to start after 1:00 A.M.; the game is simply listed as a tie.

CATCHER · IVAN RODRIGUEZ

Known as "I-Rod" by some and "Pudge" by most, Rodriguez was the rare player who seemed to get better with age. After signing with the Rangers as a 19-year-old in 1991, Pudge's offensive and defensive numbers consistently improved. His skill behind the plate in blocking balls thrown in the dirt was complemented by his powerful right arm, which routinely gunned down the best base stealers in the majors. Rodriguez was the first AL catcher to post a batting average of .300 or higher 5 seasons in a row, and in 2001, the 29-year-old became the youngest backstop ever to get his 1,000th career hit.

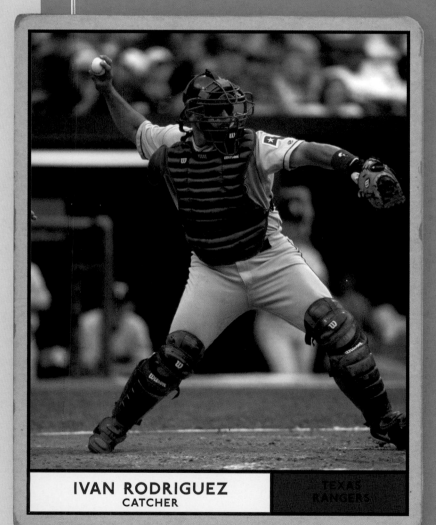

IVAN RODRIGUEZ
CATCHER

TEXAS
RANGERS

STATS

Rangers seasons: 1991–2002, 2009

Height: 5-foot-9

Weight: 205

- 1999 AL MVP

- 13-time Gold Glove winner

- 14-time All-Star

- 2,817 career hits

FIRST BASEMAN · MARK TEIXEIRA

When Mark Teixeira's name was penciled in on the lineup card on June 8, 2007, it marked the 507th consecutive game that the young first baseman had played in—a Rangers record. Although the streak ended when Teixeira strained a muscle that day, his reputation for durability and consistency was already established. The 2001 first-round draft pick spent only a year in the minors before joining the Rangers and quickly became known for the pop in his bat. He hit 26 home runs as a rookie, upping that to 38 the following year. By 2005, he was up to 43. Teixeira left Texas to join the Atlanta Braves in 2007.

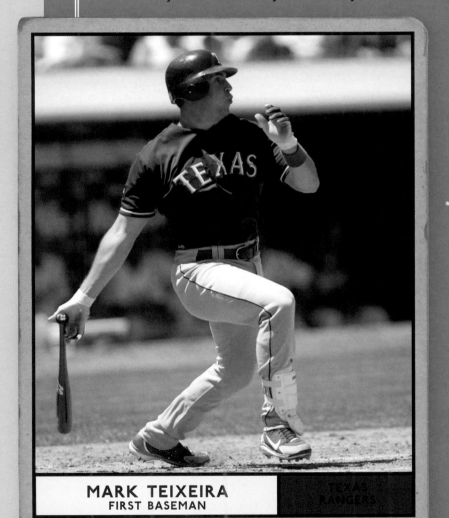

MARK TEIXEIRA
FIRST BASEMAN

STATS

Rangers seasons: 2003–07

Height: 6-foot-3

Weight: 220

- 4-time Gold Glove winner

- 2-time All-Star

- 906 career RBI

- 2005 AL leader in total bases (370)

The Vietnam War occupied people's minds all over the country but especially in the "Beltway," where decisions about the conflict were being discussed on a daily basis. New owner Robert E. "Bob" Short, who had purchased the team in 1968, saw this disinterest in the team as an opportunity to move his franchise to Texas. In 1972, the Senators relocated to Arlington as the Texas Rangers, a name Short chose in honor of the legendary lawmen of the West.

Before the Rangers donned their new red, white, and blue uniforms, Turnpike Stadium had to be expanded. The seating capacity was nearly doubled, and the field was christened Arlington Stadium. Ted Williams stayed on as skipper, and Texas fans hoped the moves signaled a fresh start for the franchise. Unfortunately, the 1972 Rangers posted an embarrassing 54–100 record. Howard was traded in August, and Williams retired at the end of the year. Replacing him took all of the following season to figure out; three different managers combined to lead the team to another miserable 57–105 record in 1973. At the end of the season, it was Billy Martin who retained control and who would return as skipper in 1974.

LONE STAR STABILITY

The Rangers figured out how to win more games than they lost during the 1974 season—and in the process, they gave fans plenty of reasons to visit Arlington Stadium in record numbers. Left fielder Jeff Burroughs's 25 long balls and 118 runs batted in (RBI) earned him the AL Most Valuable Player (MVP) award that year and a trip to the All-Star Game. The Rangers' pitching improved, too. Fergie Jenkins led the AL with 25 wins and was a close contender for the Cy Young Award as the best pitcher in the league. When later asked about his dominating season, Jenkins replied, "I didn't consider pitching to be work—I was having fun getting the most hitters out."

For the next few years, the Rangers' lineup relied on a core of solid, young players to help the team find its groove. First baseman Mike Hargrove, who earned AL Rookie of the Year honors in 1974, was nicknamed "The Human Rain Delay" for his tendency to linger at the plate for every at bat, analyzing every possible outcome, fidgeting

Fergie Jenkins's 25 wins in 1974 were the highest total of his Hall of Fame career and a figure that, as of 2010, remained a Rangers team record.

FERGIE JENKINS

SECOND BASEMAN · MARK McLEMORE

In 1986, Mark McLemore made his major-league debut with the California Angels at the age of 21. It wasn't until the 1990s, and when he was with the Rangers, that he really made a name for himself, though. McLemore became known as a versatile player whose terrific all-around game helped carry his team to the postseason seven times during his career.

Even though injuries sidelined the second-sacker on and off throughout his career, preventing him from being an everyday player, coaches always looked to McLemore when they needed someone to pinch-hit or supply reliable defense.

STATS

Rangers seasons: 1995–99

Height: 5-foot-11

Weight: 185

- 1,602 career hits

- 943 career runs scored

- 255 career doubles

- .259 career BA

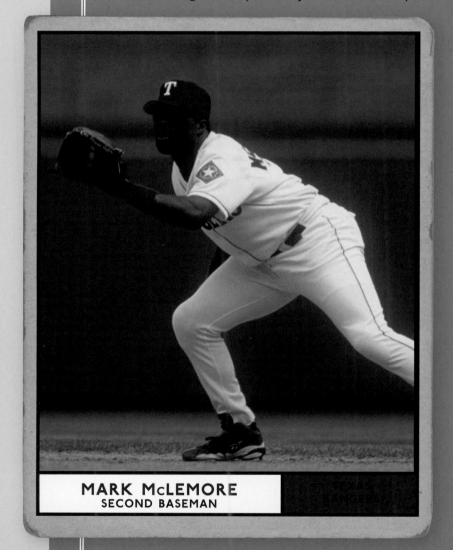

MARK McLEMORE
SECOND BASEMAN

with every piece of equipment, and generally driving the pitcher crazy. Hargrove was a source of stability for the Rangers and, in 1975, was named an All-Star. Future Hall of Fame pitcher Gaylord Perry joined the Texas crew that year, adding depth to the Rangers' rotation.

Despite the continuous improvements to their roster, the Rangers remained at or below second place in the AL Western Division (which they had joined upon moving to Texas) throughout the '70s. Team management made more moves in 1978, replacing veteran third baseman Toby Harrah with Buddy Bell of the Cleveland Indians, and hiring Pat Corrales as the latest in an already long line of skippers.

A new decade brought a new team owner, Texas oil magnate Eddie Chiles, in 1980. Bell batted a career-high .329 that year, and knuckleball ace Charlie Hough, who came to "the Gunslingers" in July from the Los Angeles Dodgers, soon became a fan favorite. Outfielder Al Oliver, who would spend 4 years in Texas without ever letting his bat cool below .309, led the team with 117 RBI in 1980. But the Rangers finished deep in the division standings, more than 20 games out of first place.

THE WIN THAT NEVER WAS

The Washington Senators' final game was played at home on September 30, 1971. The team was moving to Texas the next season and wanted to go out with a win—especially against the rival New York Yankees. In the ninth inning, it looked as if that was going to happen. The Senators were leading 7–5 as Washington pitcher Joe Grzenda took the mound to face New York first baseman Felipe Alou. The pinch hitter swung hard but managed only to dribble a slow roller back to Grzenda, who threw to first for the out. Next up was center fielder Bobby Murcer. After a few pitches, Murcer duplicated Alou's hit, grounding the ball back to the mound for an easy out. With the win apparently imminent, Washington fans began swarming onto the field of Robert F. Kennedy Stadium. The umpires couldn't clear the mass of spectators, no matter how hard they tried. In the end, the swan-song game for the departing Senators ended up being called a draw. While the team neither won nor lost the game, the soon-to-be Rangers were satisfied that at least one thing was certain—they would be missed by the hometown crowd.

AL OLIVER

For the next six years, the Rangers endured a bumpy ride up and down the standings. Corrales left after the 1980 season, and three more managers tried unsuccessfully to guide the team above .500. Manager Bobby Valentine came on board for part of the 1985 season, just in time to see the team's biggest star, Bell, traded away in July. Without the consistent play of the six-time Gold Glove winner, the Rangers fell to seventh place with a dismal 62–99 mark. In desperation, management started scouting for new talent.

So vast was the turnover during the off-season that Valentine's roster on opening day of 1986 featured 10 rookies, including pitcher

Bobby Witt and second baseman Mark McLemore. However, a few veterans remained, such as shortstop Scott Fletcher, who led the team by batting a solid .300. On the pitching front, Hough posted yet another double-digit win total while mentoring Witt and hard-throwing closer Mitch Williams. Impressively, the retooled Rangers ended 1986 in second place in the AL West, only five games behind the California Angels.

By 1989, the franchise had put together a downright formidable roster. Two rookies, third baseman Dean Palmer and right fielder Juan Gonzalez, showed special promise—Palmer for his sensational flexibility in fielding and Gonzalez for his ability to swat home runs. Power hitter Rafael Palmeiro manned first base, and newly signed strikeout king Nolan Ryan, a native Texan, commanded the mound. "My job is to give my team a chance to win," Ryan said. And he delivered. The "Ryan Express" closed the 1989 season with 16 wins, earning his 5,000th career strikeout along the way. Together, this mix of power and pitching carried the team to an 83–79 finish.

THIRD BASEMAN · DEAN PALMER

The same player who led the AL in strikeouts in 1992 (with 154) was, by 1998, an AL All-Star. In Dean Palmer's rookie year, he played all over the field for the Rangers, but by 1992, his position at the "hot corner" had solidified, and he became known as one of the AL's most consistent third basemen. Palmer's best offensive years were 1998 and 1999, when he was awarded Silver Slugger awards as the best-hitting third-sacker in the league. Always willing to do whatever it took to get on base, he even racked up 502 walks during his career.

STATS

Rangers seasons: 1989, 1991–97

Height: 6-foot-2

Weight: 195

- 1,229 career hits

- 849 career RBI

- 1998 All-Star

- 231 career doubles

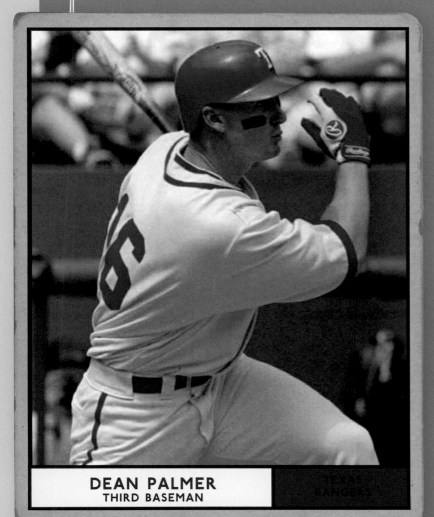

DEAN PALMER
THIRD BASEMAN

BUCKY DENT

EXTRA-INNING BLOWOUT

Scoring 12 runs in a game does not happen every day in the big leagues. But to score 12 runs in 1 extra inning? That's practically unheard of. Yet that's exactly what the Rangers did against the Oakland Athletics on July 3, 1983. Texas took a 2–0 lead in the fourth inning and held the score there until the A's tied up the game in the ninth. The teams both swung and missed for 5 more innings until the 15th, when Rangers shortstop Russell "Bucky" Dent was walked in the top half of the inning. After a single and an intentional walk, the bases were loaded. Then Texas outfielder Bob Jones slapped a double into the outfield, driving in two runs. The shaken Oakland pitcher, Dave Beard, let his next throw sail wild, scoring another Rangers run and moving a player to third. A new pitcher came in, but the Rangers were already on a roll. Before the inning was out, the team had sent 16 batters to the plate and brought a dozen of those back home as well. Texas won the game 16–4 and also set a major-league record for runs scored in one extra inning.

CHANGE FOR THE BETTER

ore standouts emerged during the Rangers' 1990 season. Outfielder Ruben Sierra, who had posted a league-leading 119 RBI in 1989, notched 96 more, and Palmeiro led the team in batting with a .319 average. Closer Kenny Rogers compiled 15 saves and also notched 10 wins on the season. Despite that fine individual play, though, the team finished third in the AL West, 20 games behind the first-place Oakland Athletics.

The highlight of the 1991 Rangers season came on the mound, as the 44-year-old Ryan hurled his seventh career no-hitter. Ryan's dominance was just one of the reasons for record-breaking attendance at Arlington Stadium that season. At the plate, Palmeiro, Sierra, and second baseman Julio Franco all hit .307 or better. Behind the plate, rookie catcher Ivan "Pudge" Rodriguez thrilled fans with his bullet-like throws to second, stopping would-be base stealers dead in their tracks. The team put together its third straight winning season but remained far out of the playoff picture.

Desperate for more than just a winning season, Texas management fired Valentine in the middle of the 1992 season. Former player and fan favorite Toby Harrah was brought in to finish out the year at the helm but was himself replaced before the 1993 opener. Palmeiro was traded to the Baltimore Orioles at the end of that season, and Ryan retired. But even with such losses, positive change seemed to be in the air.

When the AL was realigned into three divisions in 1994, the Rangers remained in the now four-team West but moved into a new home, The Ballpark in Arlington. Rogers threw the first perfect game in Rangers history (not allowing a single batter to reach first base) that year, and rookie center fielder Rusty Greer awed fans and opponents alike by diving for brilliant catches or crashing into outfield walls on an almost daily basis (including a ninth-inning catch that preserved Rogers's perfect game). The Rangers hung close to first place for most of the year. But when a players' strike ended the season in August, their hopes for the postseason faded. Technically, the 1994 Rangers finished in first place in the AL West, but since the playoffs—and hence the World Series—were cancelled, the victory was a hollow one.

When play started again in 1995, the Rangers were ready to showcase a roster loaded with more talent than ever before. Rodriguez's batting

NOLAN RYAN

Nolan Ryan's Texas roots ran deep, as he was born there and played 14 big-league seasons in the state (5 with the Rangers and 9 with the Houston Astros). In 2010, the retired ace became part-owner of the Rangers.

SHORTSTOP · TOBY HARRAH

Despite posting a lackluster .230 batting average in his first major-league season, Toby Harrah became a force to be reckoned with, both at the plate and in the field. From 1974 through 1977, Harrah found his groove, putting together 3 seasons of 20 or more home runs and posting stellar numbers in both the walks and runs columns. In 1977, Harrah and Rangers second baseman Bump Wills accomplished something done only once before in big-league history, hitting back-to-back, inside-the-park home runs. The versatile Harrah was just as comfortable playing third base as he was shortstop.

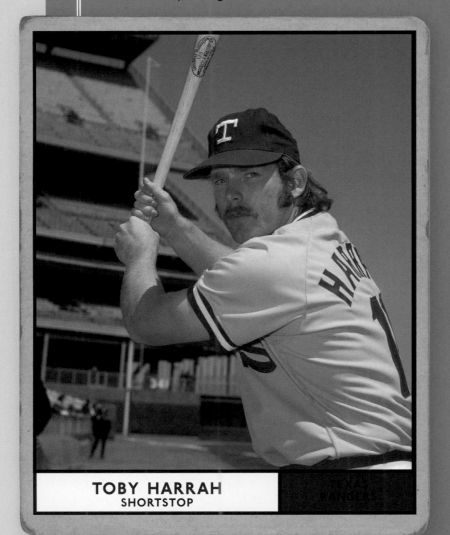

TOBY HARRAH
SHORTSTOP

STATS

Senators/Rangers seasons: 1969, 1971, 1972–78, 1985–86

Height: 6 feet

Weight: 180

- 4-time All-Star

- 1,954 career hits

- 918 career RBI

- 238 career stolen bases

WILL CLARK

average increased to .303 that season, while Palmer led the team with a .336 average. Outfielder Mickey Tettleton connected for 32 dingers, and Rogers led the pitching rotation again with 17 wins. The franchise had brought in manager Johnny Oates in hopes he could carry the team upward with his quiet, methodical ways, but the Rangers still finished four and a half games behind the division champion Seattle Mariners.

With Will "The Thrill" Clark manning first, Pudge gunning down base runners from behind the plate, and the pitching staff winning a franchise-record 90 games, it seemed as if 1996 would finally be the Rangers' year. Under Oates's guidance, the team pulled together and stayed near first all season long. As September waned, the Rangers ran away from the competition, at long last clinching the AL West title with a 90–72 record. Although it lost to the New York Yankees in three postseason games, the team set new standards for success. Longtime star Juan Gonzalez's 47 homers earned him AL MVP honors, while Oates's leadership brought him the AL Manager of the Year award.

LEFT FIELDER · FRANK HOWARD

Frank Howard's teammates dubbed him "The Capital Punisher" for good reason. In May 1968 (while the team was still the Washington Senators), The Punisher went on a slugging rampage that set a major-league record. In 6 consecutive games, the heavy-handed Howard bashed 10 home runs in 20 at bats. He was no slouch in the field, either. Besides holding down left field, Howard spent a significant amount of time at first base and in right field. The Punisher's bat remained powerful for many seasons, and toward the end of his career, he played mainly as a designated hitter.

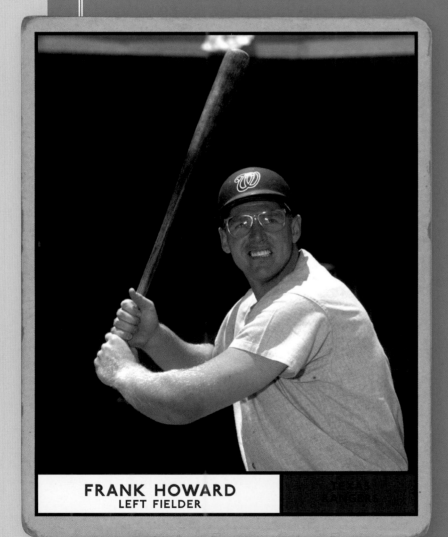

FRANK HOWARD
LEFT FIELDER

STATS

Senators/Rangers seasons: 1965–72

Height: 6-foot-7

Weight: 255

- **4-time All-Star**

- **1,774 career hits**

- **1,119 career RBI**

- **382 career HR**

A PERFECT STORY

Kenny Rogers had come a long way by the time he took the mound at The Ballpark in Arlington on July 28, 1994. He was a scrawny 17-year-old when the Rangers drafted him as a right fielder in the 39th round of the 1982 draft; he had never been to a major league baseball game and had never even pitched before. He struggled so much during his first three years in the minors that he asked to be released. But when he decided to return in 1985, he found his groove. Four years later, he was pitching out of the Rangers bullpen. Then, in 1993, the left-handed pitcher moved to the starting rotation, where he posted a healthy 15–10 record. Rogers had already won 10 games on the season by that July day in 1994, but it was the win that he tallied then that elevated him to elite status among major-league pitchers. With just 98 pitches—64 strikes and 34 balls—Rogers sent 27 California Angels batters down in order, pitching only the 14th perfect game in major-league history. "It's unbelievable that I even got to the big leagues," Rogers said later. "My life would make a great movie. It has everything, but mostly luck."

BOOMING BATS

ompared with the thrills of the previous season, 1997 was quiet in Texas. The franchise bulked up its bullpen by bringing in veteran closer John Wetteland from the Yankees, and Witt made history on June 30 by becoming the first Rangers pitcher ever to crack a homer. But the team's numbers fell all across the board, and Texas slumped back to third place.

In 1998, the Rangers' reliable hitters stayed reliable, and the pitching staff bounced back to form. That season and the next, Texas brought home the AL West crown. Both years, the team's bats were more than hot—they were on fire. Palmeiro's return from Baltimore in 1999 added 47 homers to the Rangers' offense. "He could hit .320 or 45 homers," said Rogers. "He's chosen the latter right now. He wants 45 homers a year, and nobody can complain. He does it year in and year out." Rodriguez's numbers were also on the rise, and his career-high 35 home runs and 113 RBI earned him the 1999 AL MVP award.

IVAN RODRIGUEZ

JUAN GONZALEZ

Although the Rangers struggled as a team in
the playoffs in the late '90s, Juan Gonzalez did
his part, hitting 6 homers in the 10 total games.

Gonzalez, meanwhile, remained an offensive powerhouse. In 9 seasons with the Rangers, he averaged 37 homers a year and earned 2 AL MVP awards (1996 and 1998). "He is unbelievably strong," Palmeiro said of the outfielder. "And yet has such quick hands. Even when he gets fooled [by a pitch], he can recover and then just snap his wrists—and the ball goes 450 feet."

Despite their power-packed lineup, the Rangers still came up short in the postseason. In both 1998 and 1999, the powerhouse Yankees mercilessly swept the Rangers from the playoffs in three straight games. When Gonzalez and his booming bat left town before the 2000 season, the deflated Rangers sank to fourth place in the AL West.

Broadcasting billionaire Tom Hicks, who had bought the Rangers franchise in 1998, was determined to build a championship team. So he made a move in 2000 that sent ripples throughout the majors: signing free agent shortstop Alex Rodriguez to a 10-year, $252-million contract—the largest contract in baseball history. "Our judgment is that Alex will break every record in baseball before he finishes his career," Hicks said in justification of the signing. "And he's a great

CENTER FIELDER · RUSTY GREER

When Rusty Greer came up to the big leagues in 1994, he quickly became a fan favorite. Whether he was diving for a catch or running into the outfield wall to rob an opponent of a home run, Greer gave his all in every inning of every game he played. And he didn't slack off behind the plate, either. Greer drove in the game-winning run 17 times and ranks in the Rangers' all-time top 5 in doubles, triples, walks, runs, total bases, and extra-base hits. In honor of Greer's dedication to the team and the game, the franchise held "Rusty Greer Day" on July 10, 2005.

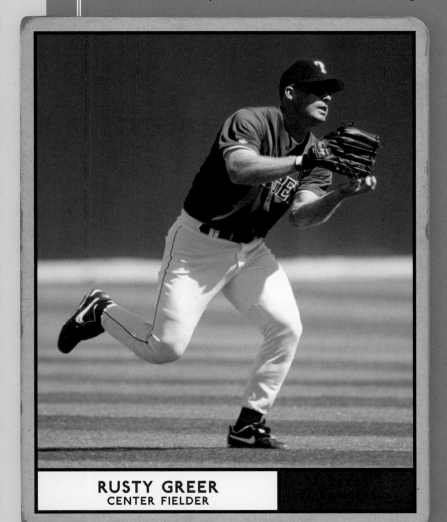

RUSTY GREER
CENTER FIELDER

STATS

Rangers seasons: 1994–2002	
Height: 6 feet	
Weight: 190	

- **614 career RBI**
- **519 career walks**
- **258 career doubles**
- **.305 career BA**

asset to the community and fans." Indeed, "A-Rod" put his bat where his money was in 2001, posting a .318 batting average, a league-leading 52 home runs, and 135 RBI in his first Texas season. But it wasn't enough; the Rangers finished 73–89 in 2001.

Oates stepped down as manager before the 2002 season, and several key players departed when that last-place season ended. Fan favorites Kenny Rogers and Ivan Rodriguez signed with other teams, while Rusty Greer retired. Despite another fourth-place finish under new manager Buck Showalter in 2003, there were a few highlights, including first baseman Mark Teixeira, who slammed 26 homers in his rookie season. Thanks to young third baseman Hank Blalock's two-run homer in the All-Star Game, the AL secured home-field advantage in the World Series, in which the Rangers hoped to appear. Yet even Rodriguez's third straight season of leading the league in homers was not enough to guarantee the team a spot in postseason play. After a disappointing losing streak in August knocked Texas out of the running, the Rangers sank to last place in the division for the fourth year in a row.

ALEX RODRIGUEZ

THE RANGERS REBUILD

n 2004, the Rangers decided to make some big changes. First, the name of their stadium changed from The Ballpark in Arlington to Ameriquest Field in Arlington. Then Texas traded Palmeiro, who soon came under suspicion for steroid use, back to the Orioles. A-Rod—who, despite his high salary, had not taken Texas to the promised land—was traded to the Yankees for slugging second baseman Alfonso Soriano.

THE REAL POSTSEASON

RANGERS

On October 1, 1996, the Rangers had a lot to prove. Two years before, they had been first in the AL West but never played in the postseason because of the strike-shortened season. In 1996, their 90–72 record earned them a postseason showdown with the mighty New York Yankees. The Yanks held the Texas boys at bay in the first inning of Game 1, then followed up by scoring the first run of the game. The next two innings, the Rangers hit nothing but fly balls and groundouts. Then, in the fourth, Rangers catcher Ivan Rodriguez blooped a single to right field, and Yankees hurler David Cone walked center fielder Rusty Greer, moving "Pudge" to second. With two on and no outs, right fielder Juan Gonzalez stepped to the plate. After a couple of tosses from Cone, "Juan Gone" cranked one out of the park, and the Rangers took the lead. Third baseman Dean Palmer followed that up with another homer in the same inning, giving the Rangers' pitchers some breathing room. New York managed to score only one more run the rest of the way. Although Texas would lose the series, it had won its first-ever postseason game—and against the most successful team of all time.

RIGHT FIELDER · JUAN GONZALEZ

"Juan Gone" rarely let a hittable pitch go by. The right-handed power hitter signed with the Rangers when he was only 16 years old but didn't become a regular player until he was 22. Within a year, he was leading the league in both homers and runs. Gonzalez's bat helped propel the Rangers to three postseason appearances and won him a slew of awards.

Gonzalez hit three homers in a game three times in his career. And in 1998, he became the second player in major-league history to rack up 100 or more RBI by the midseason All-Star break.

STATS

Rangers seasons: 1989–99, 2002–03

Height: 6-foot-3

Weight: 210

- 434 career HR

- 1,404 career RBI

- 2-time AL MVP

- 3-time All-Star

JUAN GONZALEZ
RIGHT FIELDER

TEXAS RANGERS

MANAGER · JOHNNY OATES

Johnny Oates was the most successful manager in Rangers history. His quiet leadership and meticulous organization led the team to its first three postseason appearances. Popular with both fans and players, Oates's greatest skill was his ability to recognize the potential in his players and make sure they saw it, too. Prior to managing the Rangers, Oates was a catcher for five different big-league teams and managed the Baltimore Orioles for four seasons. Oates passed away in 2004, and in August 2005, the Rangers honored their most popular skipper by retiring his number 26 uniform.

STATS

Rangers seasons as manager:
1995–2001

Managerial record: 797–746

AL West championships: 1996,
1998, 1999

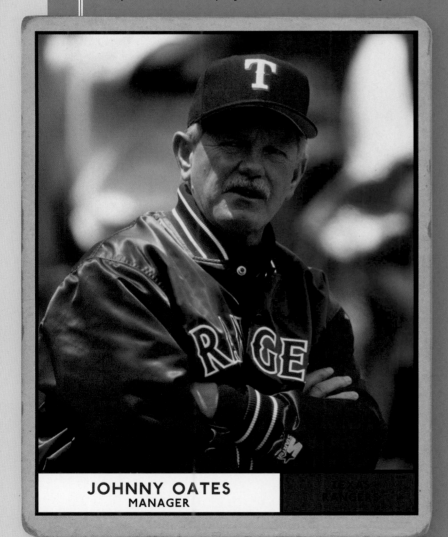

JOHNNY OATES
MANAGER

Soriano became the first Rangers player ever to get six hits in nine innings during a 16–15 victory over the Detroit Tigers on May 8. His All-Star-caliber performances weren't enough to take the team to the playoffs, but the Rangers finished 2004 a much-improved 89–73.

The 2005 and 2006 seasons were mediocre ones for the Rangers, who remained in the middle of the AL West pack. Blalock established himself as one of the game's top third basemen, Teixeira became one of baseball's most formidable sluggers—hitting 43 homers with 144 RBI in 2005—and shortstop Michael Young won MVP honors in the 2006 All-Star Game. But Texas remained out of playoff contention both years.

The most remarkable moment in an otherwise unremarkable 2007 season came on August 22, when the Rangers set a modern record by scoring 30 runs in the first game of a doubleheader against Baltimore. Rookie catcher Jarrod Saltalamacchia drove seven of those runs home, and both center fielder Marlon Byrd and third baseman Travis Metcalf hit grand slams. The Rangers even had enough juice left after knocking out 29 hits in the 3-hour-and-21-minute game to win the second contest of the twin bill, 9–7, as well. "I knew we'd get the bats going, but I never expected anything like this," manager Ron Washington said after the games. "When the faucet is on, you want it to stay on. You never want to cut it off."

Even without Teixeira, who was traded to the Atlanta Braves before the end of the 2007 season, the Rangers' offensive faucet ran wide-open in 2008. The most power came from a pair of potent players: second baseman Ian Kinsler and outfielder Josh Hamilton. Kinsler, in just his second full season with the team, led the AL in both hits and runs and had a .319 average when an injury ended his season in August. Hamilton, meanwhile, who had come to Texas in an off-season trade, had a breakout season with 32 homers and a league-leading 130 RBI. The Rangers led the majors in almost every offensive category, including a record-setting 376 doubles. Still, Texas finished the season 21 games behind the division-leading Los Angeles Angels of Anaheim.

The 2009 season was a disappointment to Rangers fans, as the club started hot before fading to a second-place finish. But 2010 more than made up for it. Texas obtained ace pitcher Cliff Lee in midseason, and his brilliant hurling—along with the steady slugging of Young, Hamilton, right fielder Nelson Cruz, and designated hitter Vladimir Guerrero—powered the Rangers to a division-winning 90–72 record. With contributions from star first-year closer Neftali Feliz (who would win the AL Rookie of the Year award), Texas then rampaged through the playoffs, toppling the Tampa Bay Rays and Yankees to reach its

JOSH HAMILTON

HAMILTON'S HOMERS

Before the 2008 Home Run Derby (part of the annual All-Star Game festivities), Rangers outfielder Josh Hamilton was better known for the addictions that had plagued his professional baseball career than for his power-packed bat. Hamilton, who was the first overall pick of baseball's 1999 amateur draft, had been in and out of drug rehabilitation programs eight times in nine years when he stepped to the plate to take his swings at the derby. But as ball after ball sailed into the stands at Yankee Stadium, his recovery finally became complete. At the end of the first round, Hamilton had tallied an amazing 28 home runs, breaking the record of 24 previously set by Philadelphia Phillies outfielder Bobby Abreu in 2005. At one point, Hamilton hit 13 straight pitches out of the park, and each elevated the decibel level in Yankee Stadium. "I got chills," he said later. "The whole stadium, the way people responded, higher and higher—you can't beat it. It makes you more focused." Hamilton was too worn out to keep up the pace in the second round, hitting just three homers and losing the derby title to Minnesota Twins slugger Justin Morneau—but he had already completed a performance for the ages.

RANGERS

A 240-pound slugger, Nelson Cruz displayed both
a powerful swing and a keen eye in 2010, clearing
the fences 22 times and posting a .318 average.

MICHAEL YOUNG

The leadership of Michael Young (opposite) and masterful pitching of Cliff Lee (below) propelled Texas to within three wins of a world title in 2010.

first World Series. The Rangers fell short in the "Fall Classic," losing to the San Francisco Giants in five games, but what a ride it was. "We just got cold at the wrong time with the bats," said Hamilton, whose .359 average and 32 homers on the year earned him AL MVP honors.

Since moving cross-country to Texas four decades ago, the Rangers have proven that they have the same grit and steely determination as the lawmen of the Old West. They've done their best to keep close to their competition, and they've worked hard to overcome every adversity that comes their way. Although it took almost half a century for the team to reach its first World Series, the present-day Rangers are determined to catch their first world championship soon.

CLIFF LEE

INDEX